Pumpkin It Up!

* ELIZA CROSS *

GIBBS SMITH
TO ENRICH AND INSPIRE HUMANKIND

For Gracie

First Edition
20 19 18 17 16   5 4 3 2 1

Published by
Gibbs Smith
P.O. Box 667
Layton, Utah 84041

1.800.835.4993 orders
www.gibbs-smith.com

Cover designed by Rita Sowins/Sowins Design and Virginia Snow
Food styling by Marcela Ferrinha and Damien Stonick Espinosa
Photographer assisted by Laura Hope Mason

Printed and bound in Hong Kong
Gibbs Smith books are printed on paper produced from sustainable PEFC-certified forest/
controlled wood source. Learn more at www.pefc.org.

Library of Congress Cataloging-in-Publication Data
Names: Cross, Eliza, author.
Title: Pumpkin it up! / Eliza Cross.
Description: First Edition. | Layton, Utah : Gibbs Smith, 2016. | Includes index.
Identifiers: LCCN 2016000413 | ISBN 9781423644569 [hardcover]
Subjects: LCSH: Cooking [Pumpkin] | LCGFT: Cookbooks.
Classification: LCC TX803.P93 C764 2016 | DDC 641.6/562--dc23
LC record available at http://lccn.loc.gov/2016000413

Contents

Introduction

The mild flavor of pumpkin seems to be popping up everywhere these days. Pumpkin adds richness and mellow sweetness to many foods and drinks, inspiring an explosion of products ranging from pumpkin tortilla chips to pumpkin ale to pumpkin breakfast cereal—and of course, the always-popular pumpkin spice latte.

The famed fruit is actually a squash plant cultivar, and pumpkin's fresh, earthy flavor comes from a long growing season and plenty of summer sunshine. There are hundreds of pumpkin varieties, and sizes range from tiny Jack-Be-Littles to whimsical Cinderellas and gargantuan Prizewinners. The largest pumpkin on record weighed more than 1,800 pounds!

Smaller, sweeter pumpkin varieties like Baby Pam, Amish Pie, and Winter Luxury are especially well suited for cooking. The large, bright orange pumpkins lined up at grocery stores and in church parking lots in the autumn are often denser varieties grown primarily for carving jack-o'-lanterns.

The pumpkin is believed to have originated in North America, earning it an enduring and endearing place in our country's culinary history. Is any dessert more nostalgic and traditional than a tender pumpkin pie scented with cinnamon, nutmeg, and allspice, and topped with a dollop of whipped cream?

While pumpkin adds moist texture to baked goods like cakes, muffins, and breads, its versatility also makes it a perfect ingredient to star in savory appetizers, soul-soothing soups, quick pastas, crispy gratins, creamy risottos, and many other foods.

Once considered a seasonal treat, pumpkin is increasingly enjoyed year-round thanks to the ready availability of canned pumpkin and the ease of making and freezing homemade pumpkin purée. These days it's easy to whip up a pot of pumpkin chili or a stack of pumpkin pancakes—or even a steaming homemade pumpkin spice latte.

I hope you'll enjoy this collection of special recipes celebrating the incomparable flavor, tantalizing texture, and vibrant color of the perfectly pleasing pumpkin. Go on, pumpkin it up!

Helpful Hints

1. When picking out a pumpkin for cooking, look for smaller pie-pumpkin varieties, which are sweeter and have a smoother texture than those grown for carving jack-o'-lanterns.

2. Select a firm, unbruised pumpkin with consistent color and a sturdy stem; check the bottom of the pumpkin to make sure the base is undamaged. Shake the pumpkin; if you can hear liquid sloshing inside, choose a different one. Smell the pumpkin; it should have a fresh, clean aroma.

3. To avoid breakage, always lift and carry a pumpkin from underneath rather than by the stem, which can dry out and snap off.

4. Always scrub the outside of a pumpkin with warm water and a vegetable brush before cooking.

5. Use a metal ice cream scoop, a serrated grapefruit spoon, or a melon baller to remove the stringy pulp from inside a pumpkin.

6. When hollowing out a large pumpkin, avoid getting messy by scraping around the sides starting from the hole opening and working your way down to the bottom.

7. One 8-inch-diameter pie pumpkin will yield about 3 cups of cooked, mashed pumpkin.

8. When buying canned pumpkin, look for cans labeled "solid pack" rather than "pumpkin pie filling," which have added ingredients.

9. One 15-ounce can of pumpkin purée contains $1\frac{7}{8}$ cups, which is equal to $1\frac{3}{4}$ cups plus 2 tablespoons. A 29-ounce can contains $3\frac{5}{8}$ cups, which is equal to $3\frac{1}{2}$ cups plus 2 tablespoons.

10. If your pumpkin purée is too watery, line a strainer or sieve with cheesecloth and put it inside a larger bowl. Pour in the purée, cover with plastic wrap, and refrigerate while the excess liquid drains away.

11. Leftover cooked pumpkin purée freezes well; wrap tightly and use within 9 months for best quality.

12. Firm, unbruised pumpkins can be stored in a cool, dry place for up to 1 month.

13. When fresh pumpkin is not available, butternut squash can be substituted.

Basic Recipes

Pumpkin Butter

Makes about 2¾ cups

1 (15-ounce) can or 1⅞ cups cooked pumpkin purée
¾ cup sugar
⅓ cup apple juice
1 teaspoon ginger
1 teaspoon cinnamon
½ teaspoon nutmeg
¼ teaspoon cloves

Combine the pumpkin, sugar, and apple juice in a medium heavy-bottomed saucepan and whisk to combine. Add the ginger, cinnamon, nutmeg, and cloves; whisk until blended. Bring mixture to a boil over medium-high heat, stirring frequently. Reduce heat and simmer for 30 minutes, stirring frequently, until thickened.

Transfer to an airtight container and chill in the refrigerator until serving. Store in the refrigerator for up to 2 weeks.

Oven-Cooked Pumpkin Purée

Makes about 8 cups

1 (4-pound) pie pumpkin
¹/₂ cup water

Preheat oven to 350 degrees.

Wash the pumpkin and cut out the top and stem with a sharp knife. Lay the pumpkin on a cutting board and carefully cut in half. Scrape out stringy pulp and seeds. Rinse and reserve seeds to make Roasted Pumpkin Seeds (page 15).

Cut the pumpkin into large pieces and arrange skin-side up in a roasting pan. Pour the water in the bottom of the pan and cover with aluminum foil. Bake for 45–60 minutes, until pumpkin is soft and easily pierced with a fork. Cool to room temperature.

Scrape the soft pulp from the skin into a food processor or heavy-duty blender, discarding the skin. Pulse until evenly puréed, adding water as necessary to make a smooth purée. Alternatively, mash the pulp in a large bowl with a potato masher or run it through a food mill. Drain in a fine mesh strainer for 30 minutes (see Helpful Hints on page 8).

The purée can be used immediately or refrigerated, covered, and used within 3 days. The purée may also be frozen in an airtight container for up to 6 months.

Steamed Pumpkin Purée

Makes about 4 cups

1 (2-pound) pie pumpkin
1 cup water

Wash the pumpkin and cut out the top and stem with a sharp knife. Lay the pumpkin on a cutting board and carefully cut in half. Scrape out stringy pulp and seeds. Rinse and reserve seeds to make Roasted Pumpkin Seeds (page 15). Cut the pumpkin into 4-inch pieces.

Stovetop steaming method: In a large pot fitted with a steamer basket, heat the water to boiling. Add the pumpkin, reduce heat to a simmer, and cover. Cook until pumpkin is tender, about 30 minutes. Drain and cool to room temperature.

Microwave steaming method: Place the pumpkin pieces in a microwave-safe bowl, add the water, cover, and cook on high until pumpkin is fork tender, 15–20 minutes depending on the microwave. Cool to room temperature.

Scrape the soft pulp from the skin into a food processor or heavy-duty blender, discarding the skin. Pulse until evenly puréed, adding water as necessary to make a smooth purée. Alternatively, mash the pulp in a large bowl with a potato masher or run it through a food mill. Drain in a fine mesh strainer for 30 minutes (see Helpful Hints on page 8).

The purée can be used immediately or refrigerated, covered, and used within 3 days. The purée may also be frozen, tightly wrapped, or stored in an airtight container for up to 6 months.

Roasted Pumpkin Seeds

2 cups pumpkin seeds
8 cups water
2 tablespoons plus 1 teaspoon salt, divided
2 tablespoons olive oil
$^1/_2$ teaspoon freshly ground black pepper
$^1/_4$ teaspoon cayenne pepper

Preheat oven to 400 degrees.

Combine the pumpkin seeds, water, and 2 tablespoons salt in a large saucepan and bring to a boil over medium-high heat. Reduce heat and simmer for 10 minutes. Remove from heat and drain the seeds in a strainer. Spread seeds on paper towels and blot to dry. Transfer to a large bowl and drizzle with the olive oil. Sprinkle seeds with the remaining 1 teaspoon salt, pepper, and cayenne pepper; toss to combine.

Spread the seeds evenly on a heavy rimmed baking sheet and roast until lightly browned, 18–20 minutes, stirring once halfway through cooking. Remove from oven and cool on the pan to room temperature.

Variation: After drizzling the boiled, drained seeds with olive oil, sprinkle with 2 teaspoons Worcestershire sauce, 2 teaspoons soy sauce, and $^1/_2$ teaspoon garlic powder in addition to salt, pepper, and cayenne pepper. Proceed as above.

Homemade Pumpkin Pie Spice

Makes about ¹/₂ cup

¹/₃ cup cinnamon
1 tablespoon ginger
1 tablespoon nutmeg or mace
1 ¹/₂ teaspoons cloves
1 ¹/₂ teaspoons allspice

Place all the ingredients in a small jar with a tight-fitting lid and shake to combine. For a single 9-inch pumpkin pie, use 1–1¹/₂ teaspoons spice mix.

Beverages and Sweets

Pumpkin Spice Latte

Makes 4 servings

3 1/2 cups milk
1/2 cup canned or cooked pumpkin purée
1/4 cup sugar
1 tablespoon vanilla extract
1 teaspoon pumpkin pie spice
1 1/2 cups strong coffee or espresso
Whipped cream, for topping
Chocolate syrup, for topping

In a large saucepan over medium heat, combine the milk, pumpkin, sugar, vanilla, and pumpkin pie spice. Heat, stirring constantly, until sugar dissolves. Add the coffee or espresso and heat just until small bubbles form around the edge of the pan. Divide among 4 large coffee mugs, top with whipped cream, and drizzle with chocolate syrup.

Pumpkin Hot Chocolate

Makes 4 servings

3 cups milk
1 cup canned or cooked pumpkin purée
1 teaspoon pumpkin pie spice
1 teaspoon vanilla extract
1/8 teaspoon salt
4 ounces milk chocolate, chopped
Whipped cream, for topping
Caramel syrup, for topping

In a medium saucepan over medium heat, combine the milk, pumpkin, pumpkin pie spice, vanilla, and salt. Cook, stirring constantly, just until the mixture begins to simmer. Add the chocolate and continue cooking, stirring constantly, until chocolate melts.

Transfer the mixture to a blender or food processor and process until completely smooth. Divide among 4 mugs, top with whipped cream, and drizzle with caramel syrup.

Pumpkin Spiced Cider

Makes 4 servings

1 cup canned or cooked pumpkin purée
3 cups apple cider, plus more as needed
½ cup water
1 ½ teaspoons pumpkin pie spice
4 cinnamon sticks

In a large saucepan over medium heat, mix together the pumpkin, apple cider, water, pumpkin pie spice, and cinnamon sticks. Bring mixture to a boil. Reduce heat to low and simmer for 20 minutes. If the mixture seems too thick, add additional apple cider. Strain the mixture through a fine mesh strainer and reserve cinnamon sticks. Pour the cider into warm cups and garnish with cinnamon sticks.

Pumpkin Fudge

Makes about 2³⁄₄ pounds

2 cups sugar
1 cup firmly packed light brown sugar
³⁄₄ cup butter
1 (5-ounce) can evaporated milk
¹⁄₂ cup canned or cooked pumpkin purée
2 teaspoons pumpkin pie spice
1 (12-ounce) package white chocolate chips
1 (7-ounce) jar marshmallow creme
1 ¹⁄₂ teaspoons vanilla extract

Line the bottom and sides of a 9 x 13-inch baking pan with aluminum foil and prepare with nonstick cooking spray; set aside.

In a medium heavy-bottomed saucepan over medium heat, combine the sugar, brown sugar, butter, milk, pumpkin, and pumpkin pie spice. Bring to a full rolling boil, stirring constantly. Continue boiling, stirring constantly, until a candy thermometer reaches the soft-ball stage, 234 degrees, 10–12 minutes.

Remove from heat and quickly stir in the chocolate chips, marshmallow creme, and vanilla. Stir until chocolate is completely melted, and immediately pour the mixture into the prepared pan. Cool the pan to room temperature on a wire rack, and then cover and chill in the refrigerator for 3 hours. Remove the foil from the pan, and cut the fudge into 1-inch squares.

Pumpkin Cream Chocolate Cups

¹/₂ cup canned or cooked pumpkin purée
4 ounces cream cheese, softened
¹/₄ cup sugar
1 teaspoon pumpkin pie spice
¹/₈ teaspoon salt
2 cups milk chocolate chips

In a small bowl, combine the pumpkin, cream cheese, sugar, pumpkin pie spice, and salt; stir until smooth. Set aside.

Line a mini muffin pan with 18 small paper candy cups. Melt the chocolate chips in a saucepan over medium-low heat. Remove from heat and set aside to cool.

Spoon 1 scant tablespoon of melted chocolate into a paper candy cup. Use the back of a teaspoon to spread the chocolate so that it coats the entire cup. Repeat with remaining cups and refrigerate for 10 minutes. Fill each cup halfway with the pumpkin mixture, using a spoon to level. Spoon melted chocolate on top of each cup so that it completely covers the surface, smoothing with a spoon if necessary. (You may have chocolate or filling left over.) Refrigerate until the chocolate is firm, 2–3 hours. Store in the refrigerator.

Pumpkin Fluff Dip

Makes 8 servings

1 (5-ounce) package instant vanilla pudding mix
1 (29-ounce) can or 3⅝ cups cooked pumpkin purée
1 teaspoon pumpkin pie spice
2 cups heavy whipping cream
Cinnamon graham crackers or small gingersnaps, for dipping

In a large bowl, whisk together the pudding mix, pumpkin, and pumpkin pie spice; set aside.

In a large chilled bowl, beat the whipping cream with an electric mixer until stiff peaks form. Gently fold the whipped cream into the pumpkin mixture until combined. Chill in the refrigerator, covered, for 1 hour. Serve with cinnamon graham crackers or gingersnaps.

Muffins and Breads

Pumpkin-Apple Crunch Muffins

Makes 18 muffins

2 1/2 cups plus 2 tablespoons flour, divided
2 1/4 cups sugar, divided
1 tablespoon pumpkin pie spice
1 teaspoon baking soda
1/2 teaspoon salt
2 eggs, lightly beaten
1 cup canned or cooked pumpkin purée
1/2 cup vegetable oil
2 cups peeled, cored, and chopped apples
1/2 teaspoon cinnamon
1 tablespoon cold butter or margarine

Preheat oven to 350 degrees. Prepare 18 muffin cups with nonstick cooking spray or paper liners; set aside.

In a large bowl, whisk together 2½ cups flour, 2 cups sugar, pumpkin pie spice, baking soda, and salt. In a medium bowl, whisk together the eggs, pumpkin, and oil. Add the pumpkin mixture to the flour mixture, stirring just until blended. Fold in the apples. Spoon the batter into the prepared muffin cups, about two-thirds full.

In a small bowl, mix together the remaining 2 tablespoons flour, the remaining ¼ cup sugar, and the cinnamon. Cut in the butter until mixture resembles coarse crumbs. Sprinkle topping evenly over muffin batter. Bake for 35–40 minutes, until a toothpick inserted in the center comes out clean. Remove from oven and cool to room temperature.

Pumpkin-Caramel Cinnamon Rolls

Makes 12 servings

1 (8-ounce) tube refrigerated seamless crescent dough
⅓ cup canned or cooked pumpkin purée
6 tablespoons butter or margarine, softened, divided
¼ cup plus 2 tablespoons firmly packed dark brown sugar, divided
2 tablespoons milk, divided
1 teaspoon pumpkin pie spice
¼ teaspoon salt
¼ cup finely chopped pecans
¼ teaspoon vanilla extract
¼–⅓ cup powdered sugar

Preheat oven to 350 degrees. Prepare a 9-inch round cake pan with nonstick cooking spray and set aside.

Unroll the dough and pat into a large rectangle. In a small bowl, combine the pumpkin, 4 tablespoons butter, 2 tablespoons brown sugar, 1 tablespoon milk, pumpkin pie spice, and salt; stir until well blended. Spread mixture over the dough and sprinkle with pecans. Starting with the long side, roll up the dough; pinch the seam to seal. Cut dough into 12 equal slices and arrange cut-side up in the prepared pan. Bake for 20–25 minutes, until rolls are golden brown. Cool in the pan on a wire rack for 15 minutes.

Heat the remaining 2 tablespoons butter in a small saucepan until melted. Stir in the remaining ¼ cup brown sugar and 1 tablespoon milk; cook over medium-low heat for 1 minute. Remove from heat and allow to cool for 5 minutes. Stir in the vanilla and ¼ cup powdered sugar; beat until well blended, adding more powdered sugar until desired consistency is reached. Drizzle the rolls with the icing.

Pumpkin Cheesecake Crescents

¼ cup sugar
1 teaspoon cinnamon
⅓ cup plus 2 tablespoons cream cheese, softened, divided
1 ½ cups powdered sugar, divided
¼ cup canned or cooked pumpkin purée
½ teaspoon pumpkin pie spice
2 (8-ounce) tubes refrigerated crescent rolls
1 tablespoon butter or margarine, melted
1 tablespoon milk, plus more as needed

Preheat oven to 375 degrees. Line two baking sheets with parchment paper and set aside.

Combine the sugar and cinnamon in a small bowl; set aside.

In a medium bowl, combine ⅓ cup cream cheese, ½ cup powdered sugar, pumpkin, and pumpkin pie spice. Beat with an electric mixer until smooth, 2–3 minutes.

Unroll the dough into 16 triangles. Spread 1 rounded tablespoon of the pumpkin mixture in the center of each triangle. Roll up the triangles into crescents and arrange on the prepared baking sheet. Bake for 11–13 minutes, until golden brown. Remove from oven, brush with melted butter while still hot, and sprinkle evenly with the cinnamon-sugar mixture. Cool to room temperature.

In a small bowl, combine the remaining 2 tablespoons cream cheese and 1 cup powdered sugar with the milk. Stir until well blended, adding extra milk if needed to reach desired consistency. Drizzle the icing over the crescents.

Pumpkin Chocolate Chip Mini Muffins

Makes about 24 mini muffins

1 ¾ cups flour
1 ½ teaspoons baking powder
½ teaspoon salt
1 teaspoon cinnamon
1 teaspoon pumpkin pie spice
½ teaspoon nutmeg
¼ cup butter or margarine, melted
½ cup firmly packed dark brown sugar
1 egg
¾ cup canned or cooked pumpkin purée
½ cup milk
1 ½ teaspoons vanilla extract
1 cup miniature chocolate chips

Preheat oven to 350 degrees. Prepare a mini muffin tin with nonstick cooking spray or paper liners; set aside.

In a large bowl, combine the flour, baking powder, salt, cinnamon, pumpkin pie spice, and nutmeg; set aside.

In a medium bowl, combine the butter, brown sugar, and egg; whisk until completely combined. Add the pumpkin, milk, and vanilla; whisk until well blended. Add the pumpkin mixture to the flour mixture and stir until just combined. Add the chocolate chips and stir gently to incorporate. Spoon the batter into the prepared muffin cups, about two-thirds full. Bake until lightly browned and a toothpick inserted in the center comes out clean, 11–12 minutes. Remove from oven and cool to room temperature.

Pumpkin Applesauce Bread

Makes 3 loaves

1 (15-ounce) can or 1⅞ cups cooked pumpkin purée
2 cups sugar
1 cup vegetable oil
⅔ cup water
½ cup applesauce
4 eggs
3½ cups flour
2 teaspoons baking soda
1½ teaspoons salt
1 teaspoon cinnamon
1 teaspoon nutmeg
½ teaspoon cloves
½ teaspoon ginger

Preheat oven to 350 degrees. Prepare three 3 x 7-inch loaf pans with nonstick cooking spray and dust with flour; set aside.

In a large bowl, mix together the pumpkin, sugar, oil, water, applesauce, and eggs until well blended. In a separate bowl, whisk together the flour, baking soda, salt, cinnamon, nutmeg, cloves, and ginger. Stir the flour mixture into the pumpkin mixture just until blended. Divide the batter evenly among the prepared pans.

Bake for about 50 minutes, or until loaves are lightly browned and a toothpick inserted in the center comes out clean. Remove from oven and cool on a wire rack for 10 minutes before removing from the pan.

Pumpkin-Maple Donut Holes

Makes 24 donut holes

1 cup sugar, divided
1 teaspoon cinnamon
2 cups flour
$1/4$ cup firmly packed dark brown sugar
2 teaspoons baking powder
1 teaspoon pumpkin pie spice
$1/8$ teaspoon salt
$1/2$ cup canned or cooked pumpkin purée
$1/4$ cup maple syrup
2 eggs, beaten
3 tablespoons vegetable oil
1 teaspoon vanilla extract
$1/4$ cup butter, melted

Preheat oven to 325 degrees. Grease two 12-cup donut hole or mini muffin pans.

Combine $1/2$ cup sugar and the cinnamon in a small bowl and set aside.

In a large bowl, combine the flour, the remaining $1/2$ cup sugar, brown sugar, baking powder, pumpkin pie spice, and salt; whisk until blended. Add the pumpkin, maple syrup, eggs, oil, and vanilla. Stir until just combined; do not overmix.

Spoon 1 rounded tablespoon of batter into each opening of the prepared pans. Bake for 8–10 minutes, until the donut holes spring back lightly when touched. Remove from oven and cool in the pan for 5 minutes before transferring to a wire rack.

Brush the donut holes with melted butter and dredge in the cinnamon-sugar mixture. Return the holes to the wire rack to dry for 5 minutes.

Pumpkin Streusel Coffee Cake

Makes 12 servings

1/2 cup plus 5 tablespoons butter or margarine, softened, divided
1/2 cup plus 6 tablespoons firmly packed dark brown sugar, divided
1 1/2 cups canned or cooked pumpkin purée
3 eggs
2 1/2 cups plus 6 tablespoons flour, divided
2 teaspoons baking powder
1/2 teaspoon salt
1 tablespoon pumpkin pie spice
6 tablespoons sugar
1/2 teaspoon cinnamon
1 1/4 cups powdered sugar
1 teaspoon vanilla extract
1–2 tablespoons maple syrup

Preheat oven to 350 degrees. Prepare a 9 x 9-inch baking dish with nonstick cooking spray.

In a medium bowl, combine 1/2 cup butter, 1/2 cup brown sugar, pumpkin, and eggs; beat until smooth. In a separate bowl, whisk together 2 1/2 cups flour, baking powder, salt, and pumpkin pie spice. Add the flour mixture to the pumpkin mixture; stir to combine. Pour the batter into the prepared dish.

In a small saucepan, melt the remaining 5 tablespoons butter; transfer 3 tablespoons of the melted butter to a small bowl. To the bowl, add the remaining 6 tablespoons brown sugar, remaining 6 tablespoons flour, sugar, and cinnamon. Mix until crumbly and sprinkle over the cake batter. Bake for 45 minutes, or until a toothpick inserted in the center comes out clean. Remove from oven and cool for 10 minutes.

To the saucepan with the 2 tablespoons melted butter, add the powdered sugar, vanilla, and 1 tablespoon maple syrup. Heat, stirring constantly, until mixture is smooth; add more syrup if needed to reach desired consistency. Drizzle the glaze over the cake.

Pumpkin Crispies

Makes 16 crispies

1 cup canned or cooked pumpkin purée
8 ounces cream cheese, softened
¼ cup milk
½ cup whipped topping
1 (3.4-ounce) package instant vanilla pudding mix
½ teaspoon pumpkin pie spice
⅔ cup sugar
1 teaspoon cinnamon
2 (16.3-ounce) tubes refrigerated large flaky biscuits
Vegetable oil, for frying

In a small bowl, combine the pumpkin, cream cheese, milk, whipped topping, pudding mix, and pumpkin pie spice; stir until smooth. Set aside. In another small bowl, combine the sugar and cinnamon; set aside.

On a lightly floured surface, roll out each biscuit to a 6-inch diameter. Spread about ¼ cup of the pumpkin mixture on half of each biscuit. Bring dough from opposite side over filling just until edges meet; pinch seams to seal.

In a deep-fat fryer, heat oil to 375 degrees. Fry the crispies, a few at a time, until golden brown, about 1 minute. Turn and cook the other side until golden brown. Drain on paper towels and sprinkle generously on both sides with the cinnamon-sugar mixture.

Pumpkin Monkey Bread

Makes 8–10 servings

½ cup sugar
2 tablespoons pumpkin pie spice
¼ teaspoon salt
4 (7½-ounce) tubes refrigerated buttermilk biscuits
1 cup firmly packed brown sugar
½ cup butter or margarine
½ cup canned or cooked pumpkin purée
½ cup (4 ounces) cream cheese, softened

Preheat oven to 350 degrees. Prepare a 6-cup fluted Bundt pan with nonstick cooking spray and set aside.

In a large bowl, combine the sugar, pumpkin pie spice, and salt. Separate each tube of dough into 10 biscuits, and cut each biscuit into quarters. Toss the biscuit pieces in the cinnamon-sugar mixture and arrange in the prepared pan.

In a saucepan over medium heat, combine the brown sugar, butter, pumpkin, and cream cheese; stir with a whisk until butter is melted and mixture is smooth. Pour mixture evenly over biscuits.

Place the Bundt pan on a baking sheet in case it bubbles over. Bake until golden brown, 30–35 minutes. Remove from oven and cool in the pan for 2 minutes. Place a heatproof serving plate over the pan, turn over, and then gently lift off the pan. Cool for 5 minutes before serving.

Pumpkin Chocolate Hazelnut Rolls

Makes 16 rolls

$\frac{1}{2}$ cup canned or cooked pumpkin purée
$\frac{1}{2}$ cup chocolate-hazelnut spread, such as Nutella
2 (8-ounce) tubes refrigerated seamless crescent dough
Powdered sugar, for topping

Preheat oven to 425 degrees. Line 2 baking sheets with parchment paper and set aside.

In a small bowl, whisk together the pumpkin and the chocolate-hazelnut spread; set aside.

Unroll 1 dough sheet on a lightly floured work surface and flatten lightly with hands. Spread half of the pumpkin mixture evenly over the dough. Starting at the short end, roll the dough up; press the ends to seal. Repeat with the remaining dough and filling. Transfer the rolls to 1 baking sheet and place in the freezer for 10 minutes to firm.

Remove from freezer and cut each roll into 8 slices. Arrange 8 slices on each prepared baking sheet. Bake until lightly browned, 8–10 minutes. Remove from oven and cool on a wire rack for 10 minutes. Sprinkle the rolls with powdered sugar.

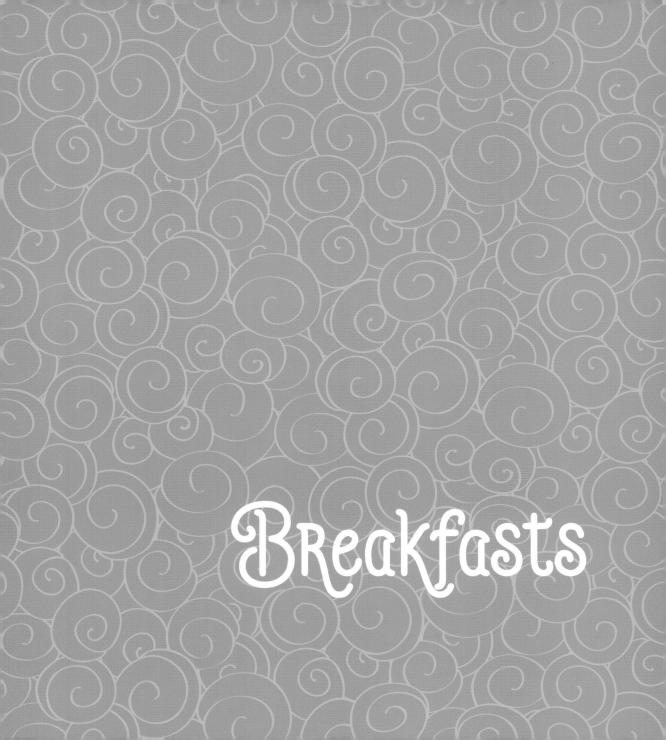

Breakfasts

Pumpkin Cheesecake French Toast

Makes 4 servings

8 (½-inch-thick) slices French bread
½ cup (4 ounces) cream cheese, softened
½ cup canned or cooked pumpkin purée
¼ cup firmly packed light brown sugar
4 teaspoons vanilla extract, divided
½ teaspoon pumpkin pie spice
6 tablespoons butter or margarine, divided
2 eggs
1 ½ cups milk
¼ cup sugar
¼ cup flour
½ teaspoon salt
2 tablespoons vegetable oil, divided
Maple syrup, for serving

Preheat oven to 325 degrees. Arrange the bread on a baking sheet and bake for 4 minutes on each side. Cool on a wire rack.

In a small bowl, combine the cream cheese, pumpkin, brown sugar, 1 teaspoon vanilla, and pumpkin pie spice. Spread half of the bread slices with the filling and top with the remaining slices. Set aside.

In a small saucepan, melt 4 tablespoons of butter. Cool to room temperature and transfer to a shallow dish. Add the eggs, milk, the remaining 3 teaspoons vanilla, and sugar. Whisk in the flour and salt; set aside.

Heat 1 tablespoon of the remaining butter and 1 tablespoon oil in a large frying pan over medium-high heat. Dip 2 of the sandwiches in the egg mixture until bread is moistened. Cook until golden brown, about 2 minutes on each side. Wipe out the frying pan and heat the remaining 1 tablespoon butter and 1 tablespoon oil. Cook the remaining sandwiches as above. Serve with maple syrup.

Pumpkin Pancakes

Makes about 12 pancakes

1 $\frac{1}{2}$ cups milk
1 cup canned or cooked pumpkin purée
1 egg
2 tablespoons vegetable oil
2 tablespoons white vinegar
2 cups flour
3 tablespoons firmly packed light brown sugar
2 teaspoons pumpkin pie spice
2 teaspoons baking powder
1 teaspoon baking soda
$\frac{1}{2}$ teaspoon salt
Maple syrup, for serving

In a large bowl, mix together the milk, pumpkin, egg, oil, and vinegar. In a medium bowl, whisk together the flour, brown sugar, pumpkin pie spice, baking powder, baking soda, and salt. Add the flour mixture to the pumpkin mixture and stir just until combined.

Heat a lightly greased griddle or frying pan over medium-high heat. Pour ¼ cup batter on the griddle and spread out slightly using a spatula or spoon. Brown on both sides and serve hot with maple syrup.

Overnight Pumpkin Brûlée French Toast

Makes 8 servings

4 tablespoons butter or margarine, melted
3/4 cup firmly packed dark brown sugar
1 teaspoon cinnamon
6 eggs, slightly beaten
1 1/2 cups milk
1 cup canned or cooked pumpkin purée
1 tablespoon vanilla extract
1 1/4 teaspoons pumpkin pie spice
1/8 teaspoon salt
1 loaf French bread, cut into 1 1/2-inch-thick slices
1/2 cup chopped pecans
Powdered sugar, for topping
Maple syrup, for serving

Drizzle the melted butter in the bottom of a 9 x 13-inch baking dish, sprinkle evenly with the brown sugar and cinnamon, and set aside.

In a medium bowl, combine the eggs, milk, pumpkin, vanilla, pumpkin pie spice, and salt; whisk until blended. Dip the bread slices in the pumpkin mixture and arrange in the baking dish, overlapping if necessary. Pour any remaining pumpkin mixture evenly over the bread. Cover tightly with aluminum foil and refrigerate for at least 4 hours, or overnight.

Preheat oven to 350 degrees.

When ready to bake, sprinkle the pecans evenly over the top. Replace the foil and bake for 30 minutes. Remove foil and continue baking until top is golden brown and a knife inserted in the center comes out clean, 10–15 minutes. Remove from oven and cool for 5 minutes. Sprinkle with powdered sugar and serve with maple syrup.

Pumpkin Waffles

Makes about 6 waffles

3 eggs, separated
2 cups flour
3 tablespoons dark brown sugar
2 teaspoons baking powder
1 teaspoon baking soda
2 teaspoons pumpkin pie spice
1/2 teaspoon salt
1 1/2 cups milk
1 (15-ounce) can or 1 7/8 cups cooked pumpkin purée
4 tablespoons butter or margarine, melted
2 tablespoons apple cider vinegar
1 teaspoon vanilla extract

Turn the oven to warm or lowest setting. In a large bowl, beat the egg whites with an electric mixer until stiff peaks form; set aside.

In a large bowl, whisk together the flour, brown sugar, baking powder, baking soda, pumpkin pie spice, and salt. In a medium bowl, combine the milk, pumpkin, butter, 1 egg yolk (reserve others for another use), and vinegar; stir until blended. Add the pumpkin mixture to the flour mixture and stir to combine. Gently fold in the egg whites.

Prepare a waffle iron with nonstick cooking spray; heat according to manufacturer's directions. Cook the waffles until crispy. Transfer to a baking sheet and keep warm in the oven until ready to serve.

Pumpkin Dutch Baby

Makes 4 servings

$^1/_3$ cup walnuts, toasted
1 cup flour
1 tablespoon sugar
1 $^1/_2$ teaspoons pumpkin pie spice
$^1/_8$ teaspoon salt
4 eggs
1 cup milk
$^3/_4$ cup canned or cooked pumpkin purée
1 teaspoon vanilla extract
2 tablespoons butter or margarine
2 tablespoons powdered sugar
Maple syrup, for serving

Preheat oven to 350 degrees. Spread the walnuts on a baking sheet in a single layer and bake until fragrant and lightly toasted, 8–10 minutes, stirring halfway through cooking time. Remove from oven and cool to room temperature; reserve.

Increase oven temperature to 425 degrees.

In a large bowl, whisk together the flour, sugar, pumpkin pie spice, and salt. In a medium bowl, combine the eggs, milk, pumpkin, and vanilla; stir until blended. Add the pumpkin mixture to the flour mixture and beat with an electric mixer for 1 minute, until batter is smooth.

Add the butter to a 12-inch cast-iron frying pan and put it in the oven. Cook until butter is melted, 1–2 minutes. Remove pan from oven and carefully pour in batter. Return to oven and bake until golden brown, 17–20 minutes. Remove from oven, dust with powdered sugar, and sprinkle with toasted walnuts. Serve warm with maple syrup.

Pumpkin, Pecan, and Maple Granola

Makes about 6 cups

2 egg whites
³/₄ cup canned or cooked pumpkin purée
¹/₂ cup maple syrup
3 tablespoons dark brown sugar
2 tablespoons butter or margarine, melted
2 ¹/₂ teaspoons pumpkin pie spice
1 teaspoon vanilla extract
Pinch of salt
4 cups old-fashioned oats
³/₄ cup chopped pecans
¹/₄ cup pepitas* or chopped almonds
³/₄ cup raisins

Preheat oven to 325 degrees. Line 2 large baking sheets with parchment paper or aluminum foil.

In a large bowl, whisk the egg whites until foamy. Add the pumpkin, maple syrup, brown sugar, butter, pumpkin pie spice, vanilla, and salt; stir until well blended. Add the oats, pecans, and pepitas; stir until combined.

Spread the mixture on the baking sheets, squeezing it together with your hands to form small clumps. Bake for 40–45 minutes, stirring once or twice, until golden. Remove from the oven and immediately stir in the raisins. Cool on baking sheets to room temperature. Store in an airtight container in the refrigerator for up to 2 weeks.

*These hulled green pumpkin seeds are available in some supermarkets and specialty food stores.

Pumpkin Pie Oatmeal Bake

Makes 8 servings

4 cups quick-cooking oats
$^1/_2$ cup flour
1 tablespoon baking powder
2 $^1/_2$ teaspoons pumpkin pie spice
1 teaspoon salt
2 $^1/_4$ cups milk
$^3/_4$ cup canned or cooked pumpkin purée
$^1/_2$ cup applesauce
$^1/_2$ cup vegetable oil
$^1/_2$ cup firmly packed dark brown sugar
2 eggs
$^1/_4$ cup maple syrup

Preheat oven to 350 degrees. Prepare a 9 x 13-inch baking dish with nonstick cooking spray and set aside.

In a small bowl, whisk together the oats, flour, baking powder, pumpkin pie spice, and salt; set aside.

In a stand mixer or large mixing bowl, beat together the milk, pumpkin, applesauce, oil, brown sugar, eggs, and maple syrup until smooth. Add the oat mixture to the pumpkin mixture and beat on low until combined. Pour the batter into the prepared baking dish and bake until hot and bubbling, 30–35 minutes. Cool for 5 minutes before serving.

Baby Breakfast Pumpkins

Makes 4 servings

4 (1-pound) baking pumpkins
$1/2$ pound bulk breakfast sausage
5 eggs, divided
4 slices stale bread, cut into $1/4$-inch cubes
1 tablespoon chopped fresh Italian parsley
$1/2$ teaspoon dried sage
$1/2$ teaspoon salt
$1/2$ teaspoon freshly ground pepper
4 teaspoons grated Parmesan cheese, divided

Preheat oven to 350 degrees. Line a baking sheet with parchment paper or aluminum foil. Use a sharp knife to slice the top quarter off each pumpkin; remove the seeds and stringy pulp.

In a medium frying pan, break up and fry the sausage until thoroughly cooked, 5–6 minutes. Remove from heat, drain grease, and cool to room temperature.

In a large bowl, whisk 1 egg until foamy. Add the sausage, bread cubes, parsley, sage, salt, and pepper; stir until well combined. Fill each pumpkin with the bread mixture to about 1 inch from the top; transfer to the prepared baking sheet. Bake until the pumpkins are fork tender, 40–45 minutes. Remove pan from oven and use a spoon to gently flatten the stuffing in each pumpkin.

Increase oven temperature to 400 degrees. Crack 1 egg and gently pour it over the stuffing mixture for each pumpkin, being careful not to break the yolk; sprinkle each with 1 teaspoon cheese. Cover the pumpkins lightly with foil, return to oven, and bake until eggs are set to desired doneness, 10–13 minutes.

Pumpkin Crepes with Brown-Sugar Filling

Makes about 10 crepes

2 cups milk, plus more as needed
2 tablespoons butter or margarine, melted, plus more for cooking
2 eggs
1/2 cup canned or cooked pumpkin purée
1 teaspoon vanilla extract
1 1/2 cups flour
1 tablespoon sugar
1 1/2 teaspoons pumpkin pie spice
1/2 teaspoon baking powder
1/2 teaspoon salt
3/4 cup cream cheese, softened
1/4 cup firmly packed brown sugar
1 tablespoon maple syrup
Powdered sugar, for topping

In a large bowl, combine the milk, butter, eggs, pumpkin, and vanilla; whisk until smooth. In a medium bowl, whisk together the flour, sugar, pumpkin pie spice, baking powder, and salt. Add the flour mixture to the pumpkin mixture and whisk until smooth, adding more milk if necessary; the batter should be the consistency of heavy whipping cream. In a small bowl, combine the cream cheese, brown sugar, and maple syrup; set aside.

Brush a crepe pan or 8-inch nonstick frying pan with melted butter and heat over medium-high heat. Pour 1/3 cup batter into pan and swirl to coat bottom evenly. Cook until top appears dry, about 45 seconds. Turn and cook on second side for about 30 seconds. Repeat with the remaining batter, wiping out the pan and brushing with melted butter between batches. Spread each crepe with some of the cream cheese filling, roll up, and sprinkle with powdered sugar.

Pumpkin, Potato, and Bacon Hash

Makes 4 servings

4 slices bacon, diced
1 medium onion, diced (about 1 cup)
4 large Yukon gold potatoes, peeled and cut in $\frac{1}{2}$-inch dice (about 4 cups)
$\frac{1}{2}$ cup water
1 small baking pumpkin, seeds removed, peeled and cut into $\frac{1}{2}$-inch dice (about 2 cups)
$\frac{1}{2}$ teaspoon salt
$\frac{1}{2}$ teaspoon freshly ground black pepper
4 eggs

In a large frying pan over medium-low heat, fry the bacon until crisp. Use a slotted spoon to transfer bacon to paper towels. Drain all but 2 tablespoons of drippings from the pan. Increase heat to medium and cook the onion, stirring frequently, until translucent, about 4 minutes. Add the potatoes and water; cover and cook over high heat until potatoes are soft, about 8 minutes. Remove lid and add pumpkin. Cook, stirring often to prevent sticking, until pumpkin is tender and potatoes are beginning to brown, 8–10 minutes. Add the bacon, sprinkle with salt and pepper, and cook for 2 minutes.

Divide the hash among 4 warm plates and return pan to the stove. Increase heat to medium-high and fry the eggs to desired doneness. Top each portion of hash with a fried egg.

Soups and Stews

Autumn Stew in a Pumpkin

3 tablespoons vegetable oil, divided
2 pounds beef chuck, cut into 1-inch cubes
1 cup water
3 large potatoes, peeled and cut into 1-inch cubes
4 medium carrots, peeled and cut into 1/4-inch slices
1 large green bell pepper, seeded and chopped
2 cloves garlic, minced
1 medium onion, chopped
2 teaspoons salt
1/2 teaspoon freshly ground black pepper
2 tablespoons beef bouillon granules
1 (14.5-ounce) can diced tomatoes, with liquid
1 (10- to 12-pound) pumpkin

Heat 2 tablespoons oil in a large pot over medium heat and brown the beef. Drain the grease and add the water, potatoes, carrots, bell pepper, garlic, onion, salt, and pepper. Cover and simmer for 2 hours, stirring occasionally. Stir in the bouillon and tomatoes.

Preheat oven to 325 degrees. You may need to rearrange the racks in your oven so the pumpkin will fit.

Wash the pumpkin and cut a 6-inch circle around the top stem. Remove the top, trim the pulp from the underside, and reserve. Scoop out the seeds and stringy pulp. Place pumpkin on a sturdy baking pan and carefully pour the stew inside. Replace the top and brush the outside with the remaining 1 tablespoon oil. Bake just until pumpkin is tender, 11/2–2 hours. Remove from oven and cool on the baking sheet for 5 minutes. Serve stew directly from the pumpkin, along with some of the cooked pumpkin.

Slow-Cooked Pumpkin Chili

Makes 10–12 servings

2 pounds spicy bulk sausage
1 onion, chopped
1 red bell pepper, seeded and diced
1 green bell pepper, seeded and diced
2 (15-ounce) cans kidney beans, drained and rinsed
1 (26-ounce) can tomato sauce
1 (15-ounce) can or 1 $^7/_8$ cups cooked pumpkin purée
1 cup chicken broth
1 (4-ounce) can diced green chiles
2 tablespoons chili powder
1 $^1/_2$ teaspoons salt
**$^1/_2$ teaspoon freshly ground
    black pepper**
Sour cream, for serving
Grated cheese, for serving

In a large frying pan over medium heat, break up and cook the sausage until browned; remove and drain on paper towels. Drain all but 1 tablespoon of the drippings from the pan. Add the onion and bell peppers and sauté over medium heat, stirring occasionally, until tender, 5–6 minutes.

Transfer the onion mixture to a 4-quart slow cooker and add the sausage, beans, tomato sauce, pumpkin, chicken broth, green chiles, chili powder, salt, and pepper. Cover and cook on low for 6–7 hours or high for 4–5 hours, adding water if mixture becomes too thick. Serve with sour cream and cheese.

Comforting Pumpkin Chicken Soup

Makes 8 servings

4 tablespoons olive oil
1 cup finely chopped onion
1 cup diced celery
1 cup diced carrots
4 cloves garlic, minced
3 cups cooked, shredded chicken
4 cups chicken broth
1 (15-ounce) can or 1$^{7}/_{8}$ cups cooked pumpkin purée
$^{1}/_{2}$ cup heavy cream
1 $^{1}/_{2}$ teaspoons salt
$^{1}/_{2}$ teaspoon freshly ground black pepper
1 cup grated cheddar cheese
$^{1}/_{4}$ cup finely chopped fresh cilantro

Heat the oil in a large pot over medium heat. Sauté the onion, celery, and carrots until tender, stirring frequently, 10–12 minutes. Add the garlic and continue cooking for 1 minute. Add the chicken, broth, pumpkin, cream, salt, and pepper. Cook, stirring often, until soup is heated through. Add the cheese and stir just until melted. Remove from heat and serve garnished with cilantro.

CReamy Pumpkin-CaRRot Soup

2 tablespoons butter or margarine
1 medium onion, diced
1 clove garlic, minced
4 cups chicken broth
3 large carrots, peeled and shredded
1 cup canned or cooked pumpkin purée
1 cup half-and-half
Salt and freshly ground black pepper
Chopped fresh parsley, for garnish

In a heavy pot, melt the butter over medium heat and sauté the onion and garlic until tender, stirring occasionally, about 5 minutes. Add the broth and carrots and simmer until the carrots are tender, about 15 minutes.

Working in batches, purée the soup in a blender or food processor until nearly smooth. Return soup to the pot and add the pumpkin and half-and half. Stir and heat through, seasoning with salt and pepper to taste. Garnish with parsley.

Curried Pumpkin Soup

Makes 6 servings

2 tablespoons butter or margarine
$1/2$ pound fresh mushrooms, sliced
$1/2$ cup chopped onion
2 tablespoons flour
1 teaspoon curry powder
3 cups chicken broth
1 (15-ounce) can or $1^7/8$ cups cooked pumpkin purée
$1^1/2$ cups half-and-half
$1/2$ teaspoon salt
$1/4$ teaspoon freshly ground black pepper
Finely chopped fresh chives, for garnish

In a large saucepan over medium heat, melt the butter and sauté the mushrooms and onion until tender, about 5 minutes. Sprinkle the flour and curry powder over the onions and mushrooms and stir until blended. Gradually add the broth, stirring constantly to blend. Bring to a boil, reduce heat, and then simmer, stirring constantly, until thickened, 2–3 minutes. Stir in the pumpkin, half-and-half, salt, and pepper; cook until heated through. Garnish with chives.

Pumpkin, Corn, and Shrimp Bisque

Makes 8 servings

1 tablespoon olive oil
1 medium onion, chopped
2 cloves garlic, minced
1 green bell pepper, seeded and chopped
2 (15-ounce) cans or 3³⁄₄ cups cooked pumpkin purée
4 cups chicken or vegetable broth
1¹⁄₂ teaspoons seafood seasoning, such as Old Bay
¹⁄₄ teaspoon freshly ground black pepper
2 (14.5-ounce) cans cream-style corn
1¹⁄₂ pounds medium shrimp, peeled and deveined
Finely chopped green onions, for garnish

In a large pot over medium heat, heat the oil and sauté the onion, garlic, and bell pepper until tender, 6–7 minutes. Stir in the pumpkin, broth, seafood seasoning, pepper, and corn; heat, stirring frequently, until mixture simmers. Reduce heat to low and cook, stirring often, for 15 minutes. Add shrimp, increase heat to medium, and cook until shrimp are pink and opaque, 4–7 minutes. Serve garnished with green onions.

Pumpkin Tortilla Soup

Makes 8 servings

1 (2-pound) cooked rotisserie chicken
1 tablespoon olive oil
1 large onion, chopped
1 leek, white and pale-green parts only, sliced
6 cups chicken broth
2 (10-ounce) cans diced tomatoes and green chiles, with liquid
2 cups vegetable juice, such as V-8 or tomato juice
1 (15-ounce) can or 1$^7/_8$ cups cooked pumpkin purée
2 stalks celery, chopped
2 cloves garlic, minced
$^1/_2$ teaspoon salt
$^1/_2$ teaspoon freshly ground black pepper
1 (13-ounce) bag tortilla chips
$^1/_4$ cup fresh cilantro leaves
8 ounces grated Monterey Jack cheese

Remove the chicken meat from the bones and cut or tear into medium-size pieces; reserve.

Heat oil in a large pot over medium heat; sauté the onions and leeks until tender, 6–7 minutes. Add the broth, tomatoes and chiles, juice, pumpkin, celery, garlic, salt, and pepper; stir to combine. Increase heat and cook until almost boiling; reduce heat to medium-low and simmer for 1 hour. Add the chicken and simmer for 15 more minutes.

Divide the tortilla chips among 8 soup bowls and gently crush. Ladle the soup over the chips and garnish with cilantro and cheese.

Side Dishes

Pumpkin Fries with Honey Mustard

Makes about 4 servings

1/2 cup mayonnaise
1 tablespoon yellow mustard
1 1/2 tablespoons honey
Pinch of cayenne pepper
1 (1-pound) baking pumpkin
2 tablespoons olive oil
1 1/2 teaspoons pumpkin pie spice
2 teaspoons cinnamon
1 teaspoon salt

Preheat oven to 350 degrees. Line a baking sheet with parchment paper and set aside.

In a small bowl, combine the mayonnaise, mustard, honey, and cayenne pepper; stir until smooth. Cover and refrigerate.

Halve the pumpkin and remove the stem, seeds, and pulp; use a vegetable peeler to remove the skin. Use a sharp knife to cut pumpkin into 1/4- to 1/2-inch-thick strips, 3–4 inches long. Transfer to a medium bowl and drizzle with the olive oil. Sprinkle with the pumpkin pie spice, cinnamon, and salt; stir to coat.

Spread the fries in a single layer on prepared baking sheet. Cook until lightly browned and just tender, stirring occasionally, 30–35 minutes. Drain on paper towels and serve with honey mustard.

Pumpkin Mashed Potatoes

Makes 10 servings

8 medium russet potatoes, peeled and quartered
1 (15-ounce) can or 1 $\frac{7}{8}$ cups cooked pumpkin purée
8 ounces cream cheese, softened
$\frac{1}{2}$ cup half-and-half
$\frac{1}{2}$ cup butter or margarine, softened
1 teaspoon garlic powder
1 teaspoon salt
$\frac{1}{4}$ teaspoon paprika

Preheat oven to 350 degrees. Prepare a 9 x 13-inch baking dish with nonstick cooking spray and set aside.

Fill a large pot with water and heat to boiling over medium-high heat. Cook the potatoes until tender, 15–20 minutes. Drain potatoes in a strainer, return to the pot, and mash with a potato masher until almost smooth.

Add the pumpkin, cream cheese, half-and-half, butter, garlic powder, and salt; mash together until well combined. Spread in the prepared baking dish and sprinkle with paprika. Bake until top is lightly browned, about 30 minutes.

Roasted Pumpkin and Acorn Squash

Makes 8 servings

1 (1-pound) baking pumpkin
1 (1-pound) acorn squash
2 medium sweet onions, quartered
¼ cup olive oil
Salt and freshly ground pepper
Chopped fresh parsley, for garnish

Preheat oven to 400 degrees.

Peel the skin from the pumpkin and squash. Cut both in half and remove the seeds and stem. Cut into 1-inch cubes. Transfer pumpkin and squash to a large bowl and add the onions. Drizzle with olive oil and stir to coat.

Spread the mixture evenly in a large roasting pan and season with salt and pepper. Roast until the pumpkin and squash are lightly browned and just tender, stirring occasionally, 45–60 minutes. Garnish with parsley before serving.

Maple-Roasted Pumpkin and Brussels Sprouts

Makes 6 servings

¹/₂ cup chopped pecans
1 (1-pound) baking pumpkin, peeled and cubed
2 tablespoons olive oil
2 tablespoons maple syrup
1 pound Brussels sprouts, halved lengthwise
Salt and freshly ground black pepper

Preheat oven to 400 degrees. Spread the pecans on a baking sheet and bake, stirring once, until lightly toasted, about 5 minutes; reserve the pecans and wipe off the baking sheet.

In a medium bowl, stir together the pumpkin, oil, and syrup. Spread on a baking sheet and bake for 20 minutes, stirring once halfway through cooking time.

Remove baking sheet from oven, add the Brussels sprouts, and stir to combine. Return to oven and bake until pumpkin and sprouts are tender, about 20 minutes, stirring once halfway through cooking time. Remove from oven and season to taste with salt and pepper. Sprinkle with toasted pecans.

Cauliflower Pumpkin Gratin

1 (3-pound) cauliflower, cut into 2-inch pieces
4 tablespoons butter or margarine, divided
3 tablespoons flour
2 cups hot milk
$1/2$ cup canned or cooked pumpkin purée
1 teaspoon salt, plus more for seasoning
$1/2$ teaspoon freshly ground black pepper, plus more for seasoning
$1/4$ teaspoon nutmeg
$3/4$ cup grated Swiss cheese, divided
$1/2$ cup grated Parmesan cheese
$1/2$ cup fresh whole-wheat breadcrumbs

Preheat oven to 375 degrees. Prepare a 9 x 13-inch baking dish with nonstick cooking spray and set aside.

Bring a large pot of water to a boil. Cook the cauliflower until tender but still firm, 5–6 minutes; drain and reserve.

Melt 2 tablespoons butter in a medium saucepan over low heat. Add the flour and whisk constantly for 2 minutes. Add the hot milk and cook, whisking constantly, until mixture comes to a boil and thickens. Whisk in the pumpkin and remove from heat. Add the salt, pepper, nutmeg, $1/2$ cup Swiss cheese, and Parmesan cheese; stir just until blended. Pour one-third of the sauce into the bottom of the baking dish. Arrange the cauliflower in the dish and pour the rest of the sauce evenly over top. Combine the breadcrumbs with the remaining $1/4$ cup Swiss cheese in a small bowl and sprinkle on top. Melt the remaining 2 tablespoons butter in a small saucepan; drizzle butter over the gratin. Sprinkle with salt and pepper. Bake until bubbly and top is browned, 30–35 minutes.

CRispy Pumpkin Potato Bake

Makes 12 servings

2 tablespoons butter or margarine
2 large onions, thinly sliced
1 cup half-and-half
1 cup canned or cooked pumpkin purée
1 teaspoon salt
1/2 teaspoon freshly ground black pepper
3 pounds Yukon gold potatoes, peeled and cut into 1/4-inch slices
2 cups soft breadcrumbs
8 ounces grated Gruyère or Swiss cheese

Preheat oven to 350 degrees. Prepare a 9 x 13-inch baking pan with nonstick cooking spray and set aside.

Melt the butter in a large frying pan over medium heat; cook the onions, stirring frequently, for 15 minutes, or until golden brown. In a medium bowl, whisk together the half-and-half, pumpkin, salt, and pepper. Arrange the onions and potatoes in alternating layers in the prepared pan, then pour the pumpkin mixture evenly over the top. Cover with aluminum foil and bake for 75 minutes.

Remove the baking pan from the oven and increase temperature to 400 degrees. Sprinkle the breadcrumbs and cheese evenly over top of the mixture and bake, uncovered, for 15–20 minutes, until golden brown.

Dinners

Pumpkin, Bacon, and Broccoli Pasta

Makes 8 servings

1 tablespoon butter or margarine
1 medium onion, thinly sliced
1 (15-ounce) can or 1⅞ cups cooked pumpkin purée
1 cup chicken broth
1 cup half-and-half
2 tablespoons olive oil
1 clove garlic, minced
1 teaspoon salt
½ teaspoon dried sage
¼ teaspoon freshly ground black pepper
1 pound uncooked bow-tie pasta
1 pound broccoli stems and florets, chopped
6 slices bacon, cooked, drained, and crumbled
1 cup grated mozzarella cheese, divided
¼ cup grated Parmesan cheese
Chopped flat-leaf parsley, for garnish

Heat the butter in a large frying pan and cook the onions until caramelized, 20–30 minutes; set aside. In a blender or food processor, purée the pumpkin, broth, half-and-half, oil, garlic, salt, sage, and pepper until smooth. Add the mixture to the onions and cook over medium heat for 5 minutes, stirring constantly; reserve.

Preheat oven to 350 degrees. Prepare a 9 x 13-inch baking dish with nonstick cooking spray.

In a large pot, cook the pasta al dente according to package directions, adding the broccoli in the last 3 minutes of cooking. Drain water and return the pasta and broccoli to the pot. Add the pumpkin mixture, bacon, and ½ cup mozzarella cheese; stir until combined. Transfer to prepared dish and sprinkle with the remaining cheeses; cover with foil and bake until bubbly, about 20 minutes. Garnish with parsley.

Pumpkin Ravioli

Makes 4 servings

1 cup canned or cooked pumpkin purée
$1/3$ cup grated Parmesan cheese, plus more for garnish
$1\,1/4$ teaspoons salt, divided
$1/8$ teaspoon freshly ground black pepper
24 wonton wrappers
$1\,1/2$ tablespoons butter
$1/2$ cup chicken broth
Chopped flat-leaf parsley, for garnish

Combine the pumpkin, cheese, ¼ teaspoon salt, and the pepper in a small bowl and stir to blend. Spoon 2 teaspoons of the mixture into the center of each wonton wrapper. Moisten the edges of each wrapper with water and bring edges together diagonally to form a triangle; pinch edges to seal.

Bring a large pot of water and the remaining 1 teaspoon salt to a boil. Add the ravioli to the water and cook for 5–7 minutes until tender.

While the ravioli is cooking, melt the butter in a large saucepan and add the chicken broth. Heat until the mixture simmers; keep warm. Drain the ravioli in a colander and add it to the broth mixture, stirring gently to coat. Garnish with parsley and additional Parmesan cheese.

Pumpkin, Apple, and Pecan Chicken

Makes 4 servings

$3/4$ **cup chopped pecans**
$1/2$ **cup canned or cooked pumpkin purée**
$1/4$ **cup Italian seasoned breadcrumbs**
$1/4$ **cup chopped dried apples**
$1/2$ **teaspoon salt**
$1/4$ **teaspoon freshly ground black pepper**
4 boneless, skinless chicken breasts, pounded to $1/2$ inch thick
$2/3$ **cup apple butter**
$1/2$ **cup Italian salad dressing**

Preheat oven to 350 degrees. Prepare an 8 x 8-inch baking dish with nonstick cooking spray and set aside.

Spread the pecans evenly on a baking sheet and bake until fragrant and lightly toasted, about 5 minutes. Remove from oven and reserve.

In a small bowl, combine the pumpkin, breadcrumbs, apples, $1/4$ cup toasted pecans, salt, and pepper. Spoon one-fourth of the mixture into the center of each chicken breast. Wrap the chicken around the mixture and fasten with wooden toothpicks. Arrange the chicken in the prepared baking dish, seam-side down.

In a small dish, combine the apple butter and Italian dressing and stir until smooth. Pour mixture evenly over chicken. Bake, basting frequently, for about 50 minutes, or until an instant-read thermometer registers 165 degrees when inserted into the center of the chicken. Garnish with the remaining $1/2$ cup toasted pecans.

Pumpkin Risotto

1 (1-pound) sugar pumpkin
2 tablespoons butter
2 tablespoons olive oil
1 large onion, chopped
3 cloves garlic, minced
1 $\frac{1}{2}$ cups Arborio rice
$\frac{1}{2}$ pound button mushrooms, sliced
7–8 cups chicken broth or stock, hot
$\frac{2}{3}$ cup grated Parmesan cheese
Salt and freshly ground black pepper
$\frac{1}{2}$ cup chopped flat-leaf parsley

Wash the pumpkin, cut out the top and stem, and scoop out the seeds and stringy pulp. Cut the pumpkin in half and peel the skin. Cut into ½-inch cubes to measure about 1½ cups; reserve.

In a large frying pan over medium heat, melt the butter and oil together and sauté the onion until translucent, about 5 minutes. Add the garlic and cook for 1 minute. Add the rice and cook, stirring, for 1 minute. Add the pumpkin, mushrooms, and 1 cup chicken broth. Cook, stirring often, until the liquid is almost absorbed. Continue stirring and adding broth ¾ cup at a time until the rice is tender, about 20 minutes. Sprinkle with the cheese and stir just until melted. Garnish with parsley.

Autumn Lasagna

Makes 6 servings

1 pound bulk Italian sausage
2 teaspoons olive oil
1 small onion, chopped
$\frac{1}{2}$ pound sliced fresh mushrooms
$\frac{3}{4}$ teaspoon salt, divided
$\frac{1}{4}$ teaspoon freshly ground black pepper
1 (15-ounce) can or 1$\frac{7}{8}$ cups cooked pumpkin purée
$\frac{1}{2}$ cup milk
1 cup ricotta cheese, divided
2 teaspoons chopped fresh basil
12 no-boil lasagna noodles
1 cup grated mozzarella cheese, divided
$\frac{3}{4}$ cup grated Parmesan cheese, divided

Preheat oven to 375 degrees. Prepare a 9 x 13-inch baking dish with nonstick cooking spray.

In a large frying pan, brown the sausage until cooked, then remove and drain on paper towels. Clean the pan. Add the olive oil and sauté the onion for about 3 minutes. Add the mushrooms and cook until mushrooms and onions are lightly browned, about 4 minutes. Sprinkle with ¼ teaspoon salt and the pepper. Remove from heat, cover, and reserve.

In a medium bowl, combine the pumpkin, milk, and ¼ teaspoon salt. In a small bowl, combine the ricotta, basil, and the remaining ¼ teaspoon salt. Spread ½ cup of the pumpkin sauce in the bottom of the prepared dish and top with 4 noodles. Spread ½ cup of the pumpkin sauce over the noodles, reaching to the edges. Top with half of the sausage mixture, ½ cup of the ricotta mixture, ½ cup of the mozzarella, and ¼ cup of the Parmesan cheese. Repeat. Top with the remaining 4 noodles and pumpkin sauce. Cover and bake for 45 minutes. Uncover and top with the remaining ¼ cup Parmesan cheese. Continue baking until bubbling and cheese is melted, 10–15 minutes. Let stand for 10 minutes before cutting.

Pumpkin, Sausage, and Caramelized Onion Pizza

Makes 6 servings

1 (1-pound) sugar pumpkin
2 tablespoons butter or margarine
$^1/_2$ cup sliced onion
1 pound prepared pizza dough
$^3/_4$ pound bulk Italian sausage
$^1/_2$–$^2/_3$ cup pizza sauce
1 $^1/_2$ cups grated mozzarella cheese

Wash the pumpkin, cut out the top and stem, and scoop out the seeds and stringy pulp. Cut the pumpkin in half and peel the skin. Cut pumpkin into $^1/_2$-inch cubes to measure 1 cup; reserve. You may have some left over. Heat the butter in a large frying pan over low heat. Add the pumpkin and onion and cook, stirring occasionally, until pumpkin is tender and onions are a deep golden brown, 20–30 minutes; reserve.

Preheat oven to 400 degrees.

Flatten the dough out on an ungreased 14-inch pizza pan and prick thoroughly with a fork. Bake until lightly browned, 10–12 minutes. While the dough is cooking, break up and cook the sausage in a large frying pan over medium heat until no longer pink; drain. Spread a thin layer of the pizza sauce over the crust and top with the pumpkin-onion mixture. Top with the sausage and sprinkle with cheese. Bake until golden brown, 10–12 minutes. Cut into wedges before serving.

CReamy Pumpkin Mac and Cheese

Makes 6 servings

1 pound uncooked elbow macaroni
¼ cup butter or margarine
¼ cup flour
2 cups milk
½ teaspoon salt
¼ teaspoon freshly ground black pepper
1 teaspoon Dijon mustard
1 cup canned or cooked pumpkin purée
2½ cups grated cheddar cheese, divided

In a large pot of salted boiling water, cook the macaroni according to package directions.

While the macaroni is cooking, melt the butter in a medium saucepan over low heat. Add the flour and whisk for 1 minute. Remove pan from heat and stir in the milk. Return pan to heat and continue cooking until mixture thickens and starts to simmer. Add the salt, pepper, mustard, and pumpkin, stirring until combined. Add 2 cups cheese and stir until melted.

Drain the macaroni and add to the cheese sauce, stirring to coat; adjust seasoning taste. Sprinkle the remaining ½ cup cheese over the top and serve.

Pumpkin Turkey Enchiladas

Makes 6–8 servings

1/2 cup vegetable oil
18 (6-inch) corn tortillas
3/4 cup finely chopped onion
3/4 cup canned or cooked pumpkin purée, divided
3 cups chopped cooked turkey
2 cups grated Monterey Jack cheese, divided
1/4 cup butter or margarine
1/4 cup flour
2 cups chicken broth
1 (4-ounce) can chopped green chiles
3/4 cup sour cream
Chopped green onions, for garnish

Preheat oven to 375 degrees. Prepare a 9 x 13-inch baking dish with nonstick cooking spray and set aside.

Heat oil in a medium frying pan until it shimmers. Cook each tortilla just until softened, about 10 seconds; drain on paper towels. Pour out the oil but do not wipe out the pan. Return pan to heat and sauté the onion until translucent, about 5 minutes. Add 1/4 cup pumpkin and cook until heated through.

Transfer mixture to a large bowl and add the turkey and 1 1/2 cups cheese; stir until combined. Divide mixture evenly in the center of each tortilla. Roll tortillas around the filling and arrange seam-side down in the prepared baking dish. In a large saucepan, melt the butter. Add the flour and whisk to combine. Whisk in the broth, stirring constantly, until mixture thickens. Stir in the chiles, remaining 1/2 cup pumpkin, and sour cream until heated; pour evenly over enchiladas. Cover with foil and bake until hot, 20–25 minutes. Top with the remaining 1/2 cup cheese and return to the oven for 5 more minutes. Serve garnished with green onions.

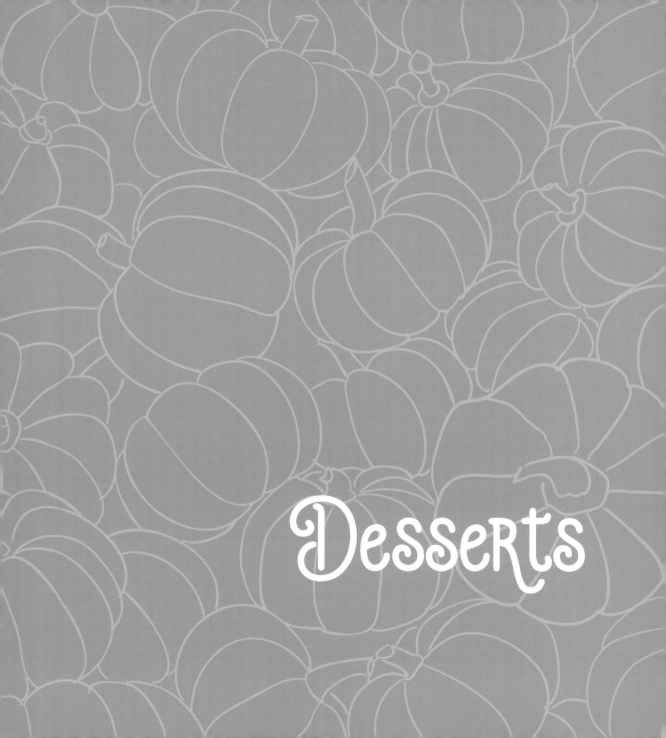

Desserts

Pumpkin Crunch Cheesecake

Makes 10 servings

1 ³/₄ cups crushed shortbread cookies
1 tablespoon butter or margarine, melted
3 (8-ounce) packages cream cheese, softened
1 ¼ cups firmly packed dark brown sugar
1 (15-ounce) can or 1 ⁷/₈ cups cooked pumpkin purée
1 (5-ounce) can evaporated milk
2 eggs
2 tablespoons cornstarch
¹/₂ teaspoon cinnamon
¹/₄ teaspoon ginger
1 (8-ounce) container sour cream, room temperature
2 tablespoons sugar
¹/₂ teaspoon vanilla
1 cup toffee bits
¹/₃ cup caramel topping

Preheat oven to 350 degrees. In a small bowl, combine the cookie crumbs and butter. Press the crumbs into the bottom and 1 inch up the side of a 9-inch springform pan. Bake for 7 minutes; do not allow to brown. Remove from oven and let cool on a wire rack for 10 minutes.

In a large bowl, beat the cream cheese and brown sugar until creamy, about 2 minutes. Add the pumpkin, milk, eggs, cornstarch, cinnamon, and ginger; beat well. Pour the mixture into the cooled crust. Bake until edge is set but center still moves slightly, about 1 hour. Remove from oven. Do not turn off oven.

In a small bowl, combine the sour cream, sugar, and vanilla; mix well. Spread the mixture over warm cheesecake and sprinkle with the toffee bits. Bake for 8 minutes. Cool in the pan on a wire rack to room temperature. Refrigerate for at least 3 hours, or until filling is firm. Remove springform pan side, and drizzle cheesecake with the caramel topping just before serving.

Decadent Pumpkin Butter Cake

1 (18.25-ounce) box yellow cake mix
2 cups butter or margarine, melted, divided
4 eggs, divided
1 (15-ounce) can or 1 $^7/_8$ cups cooked pumpkin purée
1 (8-ounce) package cream cheese, softened
1 teaspoon vanilla
1 pound powdered sugar
1 $^1/_2$ teaspoons pumpkin pie spice

Preheat oven to 350 degrees. Prepare a 9 x 13-inch cake pan with nonstick cooking spray and set aside.

In a large bowl, combine the cake mix, 1 cup butter, and 1 egg; stir until blended. Pat the mixture evenly into the bottom of the prepared cake pan.

In a large bowl, beat the pumpkin and cream cheese until smooth. Add the remaining 3 eggs, vanilla, and remaining 1 cup butter; stir until smooth. Add the powdered sugar and pumpkin pie spice; stir until well blended. Spread the mixture over the cake mix batter. Bake until edges are lightly browned (center will not be completely set), 40–50 minutes. Remove from oven, cool for 10 minutes, and cut into squares.

Perfect Pumpkin Pie

Makes 8 servings

1 (9-inch) unbaked pie crust
1 (15-ounce) can or 1⅞ cups
    cooked pumpkin purée
1 (14-ounce) can sweetened
    condensed milk
2 eggs
1 teaspoon cinnamon
½ teaspoon ginger
½ teaspoon nutmeg
½ teaspoon salt
Whipped cream, for serving

Preheat oven to 425 degrees.

Fit the pie crust into a 9-inch pie pan and crimp the edges. Fit a piece of aluminum foil inside the shell and fill with pie weights or dried beans. Bake the pie shell for 10 minutes, remove the foil and pie weights, and bake for 5 more minutes; cool on a wire rack to room temperature. Do not turn off oven.

In a medium bowl, whisk together the pumpkin, condensed milk, eggs, cinnamon, ginger, nutmeg, and salt until smooth. Pour into cooled crust. Bake for 15 minutes.

Reduce oven temperature to 350 degrees and continue baking for 35–40 minutes, until a knife inserted into the center of the pie comes out clean. Remove from oven and let cool on a wire rack to room temperature. Serve with whipped cream.

Pumpkin Chiffon Pie

Makes 8 servings

1 cup chopped walnuts
1 cup graham cracker crumbs
$\frac{1}{4}$ cup firmly packed dark brown sugar
5 tablespoons butter or margarine, melted
$\frac{1}{4}$ cup milk
2 teaspoons vanilla
1 ($\frac{1}{4}$-ounce) packet unsweetened gelatin
$\frac{2}{3}$ cup firmly packed light brown sugar
4 eggs
1 cup canned or cooked pumpkin purée
2 teaspoons pumpkin pie spice
$\frac{1}{8}$ teaspoon salt
1 $\frac{1}{2}$ cups heavy whipping cream

Preheat oven to 350 degrees.

In a food processor or blender, pulse the walnuts until finely ground. Add the graham cracker crumbs and dark brown sugar and pulse. Drizzle the butter over the mixture and pulse to blend. Press the mixture into a 9-inch pie plate and bake until lightly browned, 10–15 minutes. Remove from oven, cool, and set aside.

In a large saucepan over low heat, whisk together the milk, vanilla, and gelatin, stirring constantly until gelatin is completely dissolved, 2–3 minutes. Whisk in the light brown sugar until combined. Add the eggs, one at a time, whisking constantly. Add the pumpkin, pumpkin pie spice, and salt; continue whisking over low heat until the custard is thick and smooth. Do not allow custard to boil. Pour custard into a large glass or ceramic bowl, cover, and cool to room temperature.

In a medium bowl, whip the cream until stiff peaks form. Fold the cream into the cooled custard. Spoon into the cooled pie shell and refrigerate for at least 2 hours before serving.

Pumpkin Cream Pie

Makes 8 servings

1 (3-ounce) box cook and serve vanilla pudding mix
1 cup half-and-half
1 cup heavy whipping cream, divided
1/2 teaspoon pumpkin pie spice
2/3 cup canned or cooked pumpkin purée
2 tablespoons brown sugar
1 (9-inch) prepared graham cracker pie crust
1 cinnamon graham cracker, finely crushed

In a medium saucepan, combine the pudding mix, half-and-half, 1/2 cup cream, and pumpkin pie spice. Bring to a boil over medium heat, stirring constantly, until mixture is bubbly and thick. Remove from heat, add the pumpkin, and stir to combine. Cover and cool to room temperature. Refrigerate for 2 hours.

In a large bowl, combine the remaining 1/2 cup cream and the brown sugar; beat until light and fluffy. Fold in the pumpkin mixture until combined and then pour into the crust. Cover and refrigerate for 2 hours or overnight. Top with graham cracker crumbs.

Pumpkin Cream Puffs

Makes about 24 cream puffs

1 cup water
$\frac{1}{2}$ cup butter or margarine
1 cup flour
4 eggs
2 cups heavy whipping cream, chilled
1 (8-ounce) package cream cheese, softened
1 cup canned or cooked pumpkin purée
$\frac{1}{2}$ teaspoon maple flavoring
1 cup powdered sugar
2 teaspoons pumpkin pie spice

Preheat oven to 400 degrees.

In large saucepan over medium-high heat, combine the water and butter and bring to a rolling boil. Stir in the flour and reduce heat to low. Stir vigorously for about 1 minute, or until mixture forms a ball; remove from heat. Beat in the eggs all at once and continue beating until smooth.

On an ungreased baking sheet, drop the dough by rounded tablespoonfuls, leaving about 3 inches in between. Bake until puffed and golden, 20–23 minutes. Remove from oven and cool on the pan away from drafts, about 30 minutes.

In a medium bowl, whip the cream until medium peaks form; reserve. In a large bowl, combine the cream cheese, pumpkin, and maple flavoring; beat until blended. Add the powdered sugar and pumpkin pie spice and beat until smooth. Fold in the reserved whipped cream.

Cut off the top third of each puff and pull out any strands of soft dough. Fill puffs with filling and replace tops.

No-Bake Pumpkin Caramel Cream Pie

Makes 10 servings

1 (15-ounce) can or 1⅞ cups cooked pumpkin purée
1 (12-ounce) can evaporated milk, chilled
1 (3.4-ounce) box instant vanilla pudding mix
1 teaspoon pumpkin pie spice, plus more for garnish
1 (8-ounce) tub frozen whipped topping, thawed, divided
1 (13.4-ounce) can dulce de leche*
1 (9-inch) prepared graham cracker pie crust

In a large bowl, combine the pumpkin, evaporated milk, pudding mix, and pumpkin pie spice; beat with an electric mixer until well blended, about 1 minute. Gently fold in 2 cups whipped topping.

Warm the dulce de leche in a microwave-safe bowl on high power for 15–20 seconds, just until the mixture can be stirred; stir well. Drizzle the caramel evenly over the crust. Pour in the pumpkin filling and smooth the top with a spatula. Refrigerate for at least 3 hours or overnight. Garnish with the remaining whipped topping and a sprinkle of pumpkin pie spice.

Available at some supermarkets and specialty foods stores.

Pumpkin and Butter Pecan Ice Cream Pie

Makes 8 servings

1 quart butter pecan ice cream, softened
1 (9-inch) prepared pie crust
1 cup canned or cooked pumpkin purée
$\frac{1}{2}$ cup sugar
$\frac{1}{4}$ teaspoon cinnamon
$\frac{1}{4}$ teaspoon nutmeg
$\frac{1}{4}$ teaspoon ginger
2 cups heavy whipping cream, divided
$\frac{1}{2}$ cup caramel topping

Spread the ice cream evenly inside the pie shell. Cover and freeze for 2 hours, or until firm.

Combine the pumpkin, sugar, cinnamon, nutmeg, and ginger in a large bowl and stir until well blended. In a medium bowl, whip 1 cup cream until stiff peaks form. Fold the whipped cream into the pumpkin mixture. Remove the pie from the freezer, and spread the pumpkin mixture evenly over the top. Cover and freeze for 2 hours, or until firm.

Remove pie from the freezer 15 minutes before serving, and drizzle it evenly with the caramel sauce. Whip the remaining 1 cup cream until stiff peaks form. Cut the pie and garnish each slice with a generous amount of whipped cream.

Pumpkin Roll

Makes 8 servings

3/4 cup flour
1/2 teaspoon baking powder
1/2 teaspoon baking soda
1 teaspoon pumpkin pie spice
1/4 teaspoon salt
1 cup sugar
3 eggs
2/3 cup canned or cooked pumpkin purée
1 (8-ounce) package cream cheese, softened
6 tablespoons butter or margarine, softened
1 cup powdered sugar, plus more for garnish
1 teaspoon vanilla

Preheat oven to 375 degrees. Line a 10 x 15-inch jelly roll pan with parchment paper, prepare the paper with nonstick cooking spray, and set aside.

In a small bowl, whisk together the flour, baking powder, baking soda, pumpkin pie spice, and salt. In a large bowl, combine the sugar and eggs and beat until thickened, about 2 minutes. Add the pumpkin and mix to combine. Fold in the flour mixture until combined. Spread the batter evenly into the bottom of the prepared pan. Bake for 13–15 minutes, until the top of the cake springs back when lightly pressed. Remove cake from oven, run a spatula around the sides of the pan to loosen, and turn it out onto a clean dish towel; peel off parchment paper. Starting with the shorter end, carefully roll up the cake with the towel and place seam-side down on a wire rack; cool to room temperature.

In a medium bowl, combine the cream cheese and butter and beat until smooth. Add the powdered sugar and vanilla and beat until smooth. Carefully unroll the cake and spread evenly with cream cheese filling. Re-roll the cake, wrap in aluminum foil, and refrigerate for at least 1 hour. To serve, sprinkle cake with powdered sugar and cut into 1¼-inch slices.

Pumpkin Crumb Cake

Makes 9 servings

1/2 cup plus 6 tablespoons butter or margarine, softened
3/4 cup old-fashioned oats
2 1/4 cups flour, divided
1/2 cup firmly packed light brown sugar
1/2 teaspoon cinnamon
1 1/2 teaspoons pumpkin pie spice
1 teaspoon baking soda
1 teaspoon baking powder
3/4 teaspoon salt
1 1/4 cups sugar
3 large eggs
1 cup canned or cooked pumpkin purée
1 teaspoon vanilla
1/3 cup milk
3/4 cup chopped walnuts, optional

Preheat oven to 350 degrees. Prepare an 8 x 8-inch baking dish with nonstick cooking spray and set aside.

Melt 6 tablespoons butter in a small saucepan; cool and reserve. In a food processor or blender, pulse together the oats, 1/2 cup flour, brown sugar, and cinnamon. Drizzle in the melted butter and pulse until combined; the mixture will be crumbly.

In a medium bowl, whisk together the remaining 1 3/4 cups flour, pumpkin pie spice, baking soda, baking powder, and salt; set aside. In a large bowl, combine the remaining 1/2 cup butter and the sugar; beat until smooth. Beat in the eggs one at a time. Add the pumpkin and vanilla and stir to combine. Gradually beat the flour mixture into the batter. Slowly add the milk and then stir in the walnuts. Transfer the batter to the prepared pan and sprinkle evenly with the crumb mixture. Bake until a toothpick inserted into the center of the cake comes out clean, about 55 minutes. Cool to room temperature and cut into squares.

Creamy Pumpkin Tiramisu

1 ½ cups heavy whipping cream, chilled
¾ cup sugar
8 ounces mascarpone cheese, softened
1 (15-ounce) can or 1 ⅞ cups cooked pumpkin purée
¾ teaspoon pumpkin pie spice
2 (3-ounce) packages ladyfingers, halved
4 tablespoons apple cider, divided
4 gingersnap cookies, finely crushed

In a large bowl, beat the cream and sugar until stiff peaks form. Add the mascarpone, pumpkin, and pumpkin pie spice; beat just until filling is smooth.

Line the bottom of a 9 x 2¾-inch springform pan with 1 package ladyfingers, breaking and overlapping to fit. Sprinkle with 2 tablespoons apple cider. Spread half the pumpkin filling over the ladyfingers. Repeat a second layer with the remaining package of ladyfingers, remaining 2 tablespoons apple cider, and remaining filling. Smooth the top of the tiramisu, cover, and freeze for at least 4 hours or overnight.

To unmold, run a knife around the inside edge of the pan. Release pan sides and sprinkle with crushed gingersnaps.

Luscious Layered Pumpkin Dessert

Makes 12 servings

25 gingersnaps, finely crushed (about 1 1/3 cups)
1/4 cup butter or margarine, melted
2 cups cream cheese, softened
1/2 cup sugar
1 1/2 cups canned or cooked pumpkin purée
1 tablespoon pumpkin pie spice
2 eggs
2 (3.4-ounce) boxes instant vanilla pudding mix
2 cups cold milk
1 (8-ounce) tub frozen whipped topping, thawed, divided
1/2 cup chopped toasted pecans

Preheat oven to 350 degrees.

In a small bowl, mix together the gingersnap crumbs and melted butter. Press the crumbs into the bottom of a 9 x 13-inch baking dish. Bake for 10 minutes. Remove from oven and set aside.

In a large bowl, combine the cream cheese and sugar and beat until blended. Add the pumpkin and pumpkin pie spice and mix well. Add eggs one at a time, beating after each addition until just blended. Pour mixture over cooled crust and bake until center is almost set, about 30 minutes. Remove from oven and cool on a rack to room temperature.

In a large bowl, combine the pudding mix and milk and beat until well blended. Gently fold in 1 cup whipped topping to combine. Spread pudding mixture evenly over cooked pumpkin mixture and refrigerate until firm, about 3 hours. Spread remaining whipped topping evenly over top and refrigerate for 1 more hour. Sprinkle with pecans before serving.

Cookies and Bars

Pumpkin Chocolate Chip Cookies

1 cup butter or margarine, softened
$^3/_4$ cup sugar
$^3/_4$ cup firmly packed brown sugar
1 egg
1 teaspoon vanilla
2 cups flour
1 cup quick-cooking oats
1 teaspoon baking soda
1 teaspoon cinnamon
1 cup canned or cooked pumpkin purée
1 $^1/_2$ cups semisweet chocolate chips

Preheat oven to 350 degrees. Prepare 2 baking sheets with nonstick cooking spray and set aside.

In a large bowl, combine the butter, sugar, and brown sugar; beat until light and fluffy. Add the egg and vanilla and beat until smooth.

In a medium bowl, whisk together the flour, oats, baking soda, and cinnamon. Stir the flour mixture gradually into the butter mixture, alternating with the pumpkin purée, beating well after each addition. Fold in the chocolate chips. Drop the dough by tablespoonfuls, about 2 inches apart, onto the prepared baking sheets. Bake for 12–13 minutes, until edges are just browned. Remove from oven and transfer cookies to wire racks to cool.

Maple-Glazed Pumpkin Oatmeal Cookies

Makes about 24 cookies

1/2 cup butter or margarine, melted
1/2 cup canned or cooked pumpkin purée
1/2 cup firmly packed dark brown sugar
1/4 cup sugar
1 1/2 teaspoons pumpkin pie spice
1 cup quick-cooking oats
1 cup flour
2 teaspoons baking powder
1 teaspoon baking soda
1/2 teaspoon salt
1/2 cup white chocolate chips
1 cup powdered sugar
2 teaspoons maple syrup
2 teaspoons milk

Preheat oven to 350 degrees. Line a baking sheet with parchment paper and set aside.

In a large bowl, combine the butter, pumpkin, brown sugar, sugar, and pumpkin pie spice; stir until well blended. In a medium bowl, whisk together the oats, flour, baking powder, baking soda, and salt; mix until blended. Add the oat mixture to the pumpkin mixture and stir until combined. Stir in the white chocolate chips.

Drop the dough by rounded tablespoonfuls, about 2 inches apart, onto the prepared baking sheet. Bake until lightly browned, 13–16 minutes. Remove from oven and cool on the baking sheet for 1 to 2 minutes before transferring to a wire rack to cool to room temperature.

In a small bowl, whisk together the powdered sugar, maple syrup, and milk. Drizzle each cookie with the icing and allow to set for 30 minutes.

Pumpkin Snickerdoodles

Makes about 5 dozen cookies

1 1/4 cups sugar, divided
2 teaspoons pumpkin pie spice, divided
2 teaspoons cinnamon
1/2 cup butter or margarine, softened
1/2 cup shortening
1/2 cup firmly packed light brown sugar
3/4 cup canned or cooked pumpkin purée
2 teaspoons vanilla
2 3/4 cups flour
1 1/2 teaspoons cream of tartar
1 teaspoon baking soda
1/4 teaspoon baking powder
1/4 teaspoon salt

In a small bowl, combine 1/4 cup sugar, 1 teaspoon pumpkin pie spice, and cinnamon; stir to blend. Reserve.

In a large bowl, combine the butter, shortening, remaining 1 cup sugar, and brown sugar; beat until light and fluffy. Add the pumpkin and vanilla and mix until thoroughly combined.

In a medium bowl, whisk together the flour, cream of tartar, baking soda, baking powder, the remaining 1 teaspoon pumpkin pie spice, and salt. Gradually add the flour mixture to the pumpkin mixture, stirring until well combined. Refrigerate the dough for 30 minutes.

Preheat oven to 375 degrees and line a baking sheet with parchment paper. Remove dough from refrigerator and roll into 1-inch balls. Toss the balls in the cinnamon-sugar mixture before arranging on the prepared baking sheet about 2 inches apart. Bake until edges are just brown, 8–9 minutes. Cool cookies for 2 minutes on baking sheet before transferring to a wire rack to finish cooling.

Pumpkin-Toffee Blondies

Makes 24 bars

3 eggs
$^1/_2$ cup Greek yogurt
$^3/_4$ cup firmly packed brown sugar
1 $^1/_2$ cups canned or cooked pumpkin purée
1 teaspoon vanilla
1 $^1/_2$ cups flour
1 teaspoon baking powder
$^1/_2$ teaspoon baking soda
$^1/_2$ teaspoon cinnamon
$^1/_4$ teaspoon salt
1 cup toffee bits
Caramel topping, for serving

Preheat oven to 350 degrees. Prepare a 9 x 13-inch baking dish with nonstick cooking spray and set aside.

In a large bowl, whisk together the eggs, yogurt, and brown sugar until well blended. Add the pumpkin and vanilla and stir until combined. In a medium bowl, whisk together the flour, baking powder, baking soda, cinnamon, and salt until well combined. Add the flour mixture to the pumpkin mixture and stir until blended. Fold in the toffee bits and then spread the batter in the prepared baking dish. Bake for 40 minutes, or until edges are just beginning to brown and a toothpick inserted into the center comes out clean. Remove from oven, cool on a wire rack for 10 minutes, and cut into bars. Drizzle bars with caramel topping just before serving.

Pumpkin Gingersnaps

½ cup butter or margarine, softened
1 cup sugar, plus more for rolling the cookies
½ cup canned or cooked pumpkin purée
¼ cup molasses
1 egg
1 teaspoon vanilla
2 ⅓ cups flour
2 teaspoons baking soda
2 teaspoons cinnamon
1 ½ teaspoons ginger
½ teaspoon cloves
½ teaspoon salt

In a large bowl, beat the butter and sugar until creamy. Add the pumpkin, molasses, egg, and vanilla; mix until well combined. In a medium bowl, whisk together the flour, baking soda, cinnamon, ginger, cloves, and salt. Add the flour mixture to the pumpkin mixture and stir until combined. Cover the bowl and refrigerate the dough for at least 1 hour.

Preheat oven to 350 degrees and line a baking sheet with parchment paper.

Fill a small bowl with sugar. Roll the dough into 1½-inch balls and coat with the sugar. Arrange the balls about 2 inches apart on the prepared baking sheet. Bake until cookies are set at the edges and cracked but still soft, 10–13 minutes. Remove from oven and cool on a wire rack.

Mini Pumpkin Whoopie Pies

2 cups flour
1 teaspoon baking powder
1 teaspoon baking soda
1 1/2 teaspoons cinnamon, divided
1/2 teaspoon ginger
1/2 teaspoon salt
1/4 cup plus 6 tablespoons butter or margarine, softened, divided
1 1/4 cups sugar
2 eggs, lightly beaten
1 cup canned or cooked pumpkin purée
1 1/2 teaspoons vanilla, divided
4 ounces cream cheese, softened
1 1/2 cups powdered sugar

Preheat oven to 350 degrees. Line 4 baking sheets with parchment paper and set aside.

In a medium bowl, whisk together the flour, baking powder, baking soda, 1 teaspoon cinnamon, ginger, and salt. In a large bowl, combine 1/4 cup butter and the sugar; beat for 2 minutes until creamy. Beat in the eggs one at a time. Add the pumpkin and 1 teaspoon vanilla; beat until smooth. Add the flour mixture and stir until combined. Drop the dough by heaping teaspoonfuls, about 2 inches apart, onto the prepared baking sheets. Bake for 10–13 minutes, until cookies are springy to the touch. Remove from oven and cool for 5 minutes. Transfer cookies to wire racks to cool completely.

In a medium bowl, combine the cream cheese, remaining 6 tablespoons butter, remaining 1/2 teaspoon vanilla, and remaining 1/2 teaspoon cinnamon; beat until smooth. Gradually beat in the powdered sugar until light and fluffy. Spread a heaping teaspoon of the cream cheese mixture on the flat side of one cookie; top with a second cookie. Repeat until all of the cookies and filling are used. Store, covered, in refrigerator.

Pumpkin Bars with Cream Cheese Frosting

Makes 24 bars

4 eggs
1 2/3 cups sugar
1 cup vegetable oil
1 (15-ounce) can or 1 7/8 cups cooked pumpkin purée
2 cups flour
2 teaspoons cinnamon
2 teaspoons baking powder
1 teaspoon baking soda
1 teaspoon salt
1/2 teaspoon ginger
1 (8-ounce) package cream cheese, softened
1/2 cup butter or margarine, softened
1 teaspoon vanilla
2 cups powdered sugar

Preheat oven to 325 degrees. Prepare a 9 x 13-inch baking pan with nonstick cooking spray and set aside.

In a large bowl, combine the eggs, sugar, oil, and pumpkin; beat until light and fluffy. In a medium bowl, whisk together the flour, cinnamon, baking powder, baking soda, salt, and ginger. Add the flour mixture to the pumpkin mixture and mix until thoroughly combined and smooth. Spread the batter in the prepared pan and bake for 45–50 minutes, until a toothpick inserted into the center comes out clean. Remove from oven and cool to room temperature.

In a medium bowl, beat together the cream cheese, butter, and vanilla until smooth. Add the powdered sugar and mix until combined. Spread the frosting evenly over the bars and cut into 1 1/2 x 3-inch rectangles.

Six-Layer Pumpkin-Ginger Bars

Makes 16 bars

2 cups gingersnap crumbs
¹/₂ cup butter or margarine, melted
1 (14-ounce) can sweetened condensed milk
³/₄ cup canned or cooked pumpkin purée
1 teaspoon cinnamon
¹/₄ teaspoon nutmeg
³/₄ cup white chocolate chips
³/₄ cup butterscotch chips
1 cup coarsely chopped pecans
1 ¹/₂ cups sweetened shredded coconut

Preheat oven to 350 degrees. Line an 8 x 8-inch pan with aluminum foil, leaving 1 inch of overhang on opposite sides. Prepare with nonstick cooking spray and set aside.

In a small bowl, combine the gingersnap crumbs and melted butter and stir until well blended. Press the mixture evenly into the bottom of the prepared pan. In another small bowl, combine the condensed milk, pumpkin, cinnamon, and nutmeg; stir until blended. Pour the pumpkin mixture over the gingersnap crust. Sprinkle evenly with the white chocolate chips, followed by the butterscotch chips, pecans, and coconut. Bake for 25–35 minutes, until coconut is lightly browned. Remove from oven and cool in pan to room temperature. Refrigerate until firm. Use foil to lift bars from pan and then cut into 2-inch squares.

Pumpkin Pecan Pie Bars

Makes 12 bars

1 cup flour
1/2 cup quick-cooking oats
1 cup firmly packed dark brown sugar, divided
1/2 cup plus 2 tablespoons butter or margarine, softened, divided
3/4 teaspoon salt, divided
1 (15-ounce) can or 1 7/8 cups cooked pumpkin purée
1 (12-ounce) can evaporated milk
2 eggs
3/4 cup sugar
1 teaspoon vanilla
2 teaspoons pumpkin pie spice
1/2 cup chopped pecans

Preheat oven to 350 degrees. Prepare a 9 x 13-inch baking pan with nonstick cooking spray and set aside.

In a large bowl, combine the flour, oats, 1/2 cup brown sugar, 1/2 cup butter, and 1/4 teaspoon salt. Stir until combined (mixture will be crumbly) and press into the prepared pan. Bake for 15 minutes. Remove from oven, transfer pan to a wire rack, and allow to cool. Do not turn off oven.

In a medium bowl, combine the pumpkin, evaporated milk, eggs, sugar, vanilla, remaining 1/2 teaspoon salt, and pumpkin pie spice; beat well. Pour into the cooled crust and bake for 20 minutes.

In a small bowl, combine the pecans, 1/2 cup brown sugar, and remaining 2 tablespoons butter; sprinkle over pumpkin filling. Return to oven and bake for 15–20 minutes, until filling is set. Cool in pan on wire rack and then cut into bars.

Pumpkin Chocolate Swirl Brownies

Makes 36 brownies

3 ounces cream cheese, softened
¾ cup plus 1 tablespoon butter or margarine, softened, divided
2¾ cups sugar, divided
5 eggs
1 cup canned or cooked pumpkin purée
3 teaspoons vanilla, divided
½ teaspoon cinnamon
¼ teaspoon ginger
1¼ cups plus 1 tablespoon flour, divided
¾ teaspoon baking powder
½ teaspoon salt
6 ounces unsweetened baking chocolate, chopped
¼ cup milk

Preheat oven to 325 degrees. Prepare a 9 x 13-inch baking pan with nonstick cooking spray and set aside.

In a medium bowl, beat the cream cheese and 1 tablespoon butter for 30 seconds. Add ½ cup sugar and beat to combine. Beat in 1 egg, pumpkin, 1 teaspoon vanilla, cinnamon, and ginger. Stir in 1 tablespoon flour and reserve.

In a small bowl, whisk together 1¼ cups flour, baking powder, and salt. In a large saucepan over low heat, combine the chocolate and remaining ¾ cup butter. Heat until melted and smooth, stirring occasionally. Gradually add the remaining 2¼ cups sugar, beating just until combined. Beat in the remaining 4 eggs one at a time. Add the milk and remaining 2 teaspoons vanilla. Gradually add the flour mixture and stir just until combined. Spread the chocolate mixture evenly in the bottom of the prepared pan. Spoon the cream cheese mixture in mounds on top and swirl into the chocolate batter. Bake until center is just set, about 60 minutes. Remove from oven, allow to cool in the pan, and cut into squares.

Pumpkin Biscotti

3 1/2 cups flour
2 teaspoons baking powder
1/2 teaspoon salt
2 teaspoons pumpkin pie spice
2 eggs
1 1/2 cups firmly packed light brown sugar
1/2 cup canned or cooked pumpkin purée
1 tablespoon vanilla
1 1/4 cups chopped, toasted pecans
1/4 cup melted white chocolate, for drizzling or dipping

Preheat oven to 350 degrees. Line a baking sheet with parchment paper, fill a spray bottle with tepid water, and set both aside.

In a medium bowl, whisk together the flour, baking powder, salt, and pumpkin pie spice. In a large bowl, combine the eggs, brown sugar, pumpkin, and vanilla; beat until well blended, about 2 minutes. Add the flour mixture and pecans to the pumpkin mixture and stir to blend (mixture will be crumbly).

On a lightly floured surface, divide the dough in half and shape each into a 3 x 10-inch loaf. Arrange dough on prepared baking sheet. Bake until just firm to the touch, 25–30 minutes. Remove from oven and cool for 5 minutes.

Decrease oven temperature to 325 degrees.

Use the spray bottle to moisten the top and sides of the loaves. Transfer loaves to a cutting board, and use a serrated knife to cut loaves into 1/2-inch thick slices. Arrange slices in a single layer on the baking sheet. Bake until firm, about 20 minutes, turning slices over halfway through baking. Remove from oven, cool on a wire rack to room temperature, and then drizzle biscotti with the white chocolate.

Index

About the Author

Eliza Cross is an award-winning writer and the author of several books, including *101 Things to Do with Bacon* and *101 Things to Do with a Pickle.* She develops recipes and styles cuisine for corporate and print media, and blogs about food, gardening, and sustainable living at *happysimpleliving.com.* She lives with her family in Centennial, Colorado.

Metric Conversion Chart

VOLUME MEASUREMENTS		WEIGHT MEASUREMENTS		TEMPERATURE CONVERSION	
U.S.	Metric	U.S.	Metric	Fahrenheit	Celsius
1 teaspoon	5 ml	½ ounce	15 g	250	120
1 tablespoon	15 ml	1 ounce	30 g	300	150
¼ cup	60 ml	3 ounces	90 g	325	160
⅓ cup	75 ml	4 ounces	115 g	350	180
½ cup	125 ml	8 ounces	225 g	375	190
⅔ cup	150 ml	12 ounces	350 g	400	200
¾ cup	175 ml	1 pound	450 g	425	220
1 cup	250 ml	2¼ pounds	1 kg	450	230